As I Have Loved You

A Resource for

Small Group Faith Sharing

By Christopher J. Ruff, M.A., S.T.L.

- Discipleship Series -

Novo Millennio Press

As I Have Loved You

Novo Millennio Press
PO Box 160
La Crescent, MN 55947
www.novomill.com

Nihil obstat: Rev. Samuel A. Martin, S.T.L.
                  Censor Librorum

Imprimatur: Jerome E. Listecki, D.D., J.C.D.
                  Bishop of La Crosse
                  April 2, 2008

The *nihil obstat* and *imprimatur* are official declarations that a book or pamphlet is free of doctrinal or moral error. No implication is contained therein that those who have granted the *nihil obstat* and *imprimatur* agree with the contents, opinions, or statements expressed.

Unless otherwise noted, Scripture quotations are from The Catholic Edition of the Revised Standard Version of the Bible, copyright © 1965, 1966 National Council of the Churches of Christ in the United States of America. Used by permission. All rights reserved.

Excerpts from the English translation of the *Catechism of the Catholic Church* for use in the United States of America copyright © 1994, United States Catholic Conference, Inc. - Libreria Editrice Vaticana. Used with Permission.

Quotations from St. Thérèse of Lisieux are from *The Story of a Soul*, T.N. Taylor, ed. (Burns, Oates & Washbourne, London, copyright © 1912).

Cover Art:
Giotto. Jesus Washes the Feet of the Disciples (det.), c. 1305. Scrovegni Chapel. Padua, Italy. Photo used with permission from: Michael Olteanu, Executive Director, Christus Rex, Inc. http://www.christusrex.org.

Graphics and Design:
Alice J. Andersen
www.alicejandersen.com.

Foreword

In the summer of 2006, Christopher Ruff, director of the Office of Ministries and Social Concerns for our diocese, came to me with a proposal. He wanted to develop a diocesan small group faith-sharing program that would take the typical "Bible study" ingredients of prayer, reflective study and fellowship, and add one more—loving service.

Chris felt too many Catholics saw ministry to the suffering and needy as belonging only to Church social justice committees and institutions like Catholic Charities, with their own role reduced to giving these groups financial support. Of course it is true that Jesus tells the story of a Samaritan who gave money to an innkeeper for the care of a beaten man—but not before compassion had moved the Samaritan personally to clean the man's wounds with oil and wine and to lift him onto his own animal to bring him to that inn.

With this kind of love of neighbor in mind, Chris looked for a faith-sharing resource that would combine a prayerful, contemplative spirit with the universal call to serve Christ in "the least of his brethren." He wanted to find something that penetrated to the heart of the Gospel but that was concise,

3

readable and workable for people with busy lives. Even the vital service component had to be manageable and broad enough to include various kinds of service. In the end, Chris decided to write his own resource, on his own time so he could publish it. He then wrote a second book, with a third in the works and more planned.

The response in the Diocese of La Crosse has been extraordinary.

In what was supposed to be a small pilot phase in Lent of 2007, over one thousand people in more than thirty parishes took part (in our modest Wisconsin diocese of 165 parishes). Concluding surveys reflected great enthusiasm and more than 95% said they wished to continue with the next resource. As the program was made available to the entire diocese with the second book in the fall of 2007, nearly two thousand people joined groups in close to one hundred parishes.

This expanding set of faith-sharing resources is aptly named the Discipleship Series. I am seeing it form disciples in our diocese—integral and authentic disciples growing in love of God and love of neighbor. It is my hope that in the planting and nurturing brought about through this Discipleship Series, we will look forward to a harvest of apostolic works. I recommend it wholeheartedly to individuals, groups, parishes and other dioceses that wish to foster a deeper discipleship in Christ, so that the surrounding world may be moved to say, as it did of the first Christians: "See how they love one another!"

Most Rev. Jerome E. Listecki
Archbishop of Milwaukee
(Written in 2008 as Bishop of La Crosse)

Acknowledgments

I would like gratefully to acknowledge the following colleagues for their creative ideas and prayerful support toward the creation of this resource:

Jeff Heinzen
Ann Lankford
Christopher Rogers
Deacon Richard Sage

I would also like to thank Alice Andersen for her skilled editing and design.

Finally, and most of all, I would like to thank my wife Clare, whose love for Christ shines out, and who has been so patient with my late nights on this project.

Christopher Ruff

Table of Contents

Introduction

In twenty years of parish and diocesan work in the Church, I have experienced nothing so powerful as small group faith sharing for personal and community renewal.

Certainly the center of our Christian life is the Mass, the Eucharist, but that does not remove the human need to form "family" clusters, joining together and lifting up minds and hearts. It is my experience that such groups, if run with a certain simplicity and respect for busy schedules, become woven into the very fabric of life. Faith penetrates homes and friendships, and the Sunday Eucharist itself is profoundly enriched. These groups often remain together indefinitely.

The goals of the Discipleship Series of faith-sharing resources are to provide a framework for people to draw closer to Jesus in prayer and conversion, to share the treasures of our faith, to grow in bonds of friendship, and to serve Christ in others. In short:

- Prayer
- Reflection
- Fellowship
- Service

The first three components are common to virtually all faith-sharing resources. The fourth component, service, is included in the conviction that we are not truly disciples of Christ until we take seriously his words: "Truly, I say to you, as you did it to one of the least of these my brethren, you did it to me" *(Matthew 25:40).* Clearly the early Christian communities embraced this call, as witnessed in the words of the surrounding pagans: "See how they love one another!"

This resource contains six brief sessions. The materials for each session include Scripture passages, commentary, real-life anecdotes and illustrations, relevant quotes from the *Catechism of the Catholic Church,* excerpts from papal writings, and questions for group discussion. Each session also opens and closes with prayer.

Finally, while this resource has been designed for faith-sharing groups, it could be very fruitful for individual use as well.

May God bless you as you go forward in his name, that you might experience the fullness of Christ's joy! *(cf., John 15:11).*

Christopher Ruff

How to Use This Book

The Discipleship Series of faith-sharing materials aims to be simple and flexible. What follows is everything you need to know to move forward:

Establishing and Running One or More Groups

- Through personal invitation or parish announcements, form one or more small groups (5-12 people each).

- If established for Lent, the groups should meet weekly. Otherwise, once a month tends to be more workable for most people's schedules. Typical length for a session is about 90 minutes. Whatever time frame is established, it should be rigorously respected.

- Each group should have a facilitator. It can be the same person at each meeting, or the facilitator role can rotate.

- The job of the facilitator is not to be an expert in the material or to do a lot of talking. Rather, it is to start and end the meeting on time, to help keep things moving and on topic, and to foster a friendly, supportive environment in which everyone feels invited to contribute.

- The group members decide where they would like to meet. It is ideal to hold the sessions in each other's homes since a key goal is to bring faith into daily life. If this is not workable, a room on church grounds is fine, or some combination of the two.

- Each member is expected to read the material prayerfully ahead of the session, jotting a few notes in response to the "Questions for Discussion."

- The session begins with the Prayer to the Holy Spirit or some other appropriate prayer so that hearts may be opened to God's presence.

- The group members then read aloud the material for that session, taking turns reading a paragraph or small section. This pattern should continue all the way through the discussion questions.

- When there are about ten minutes left in the allotted schedule, it is time to proceed to the "Group Prayers of Intercession," even if the group has not finished all the discussion questions.

- The prayers of intercession are intended to be spontaneous prayer intentions. They direct the power of prayer to various needs and simultaneously deepen the spirit of fellowship in the group. Conclude with the "Closing Prayer."

- The session should end on time, even if members are eager to keep going. This is vital for the health and longevity of the group. It is good to follow with fifteen or twenty minutes of social time for those who are able to stay. Simple refreshments are a nice touch, with emphasis on the word simple; otherwise, people feel pressure to keep up with high expectations.

The Service Component

- The Service Component distinguishes this program from many other faith-sharing approaches. It is anticipated that group members will devote an hour or two to some form of service between sessions (if meetings are weekly, this could be an hour or two each month). The service may be carried out individually or together with others.

- Service can take many forms, but it should come from the heart. Certainly service to the poor, the sick, the elderly, the homebound, the homeless, etc., has always had a privileged place for Christ's followers.

- Some may already be devoting a great deal of time to service. In that case, it is enough to consciously "dedicate" some portion of that service to the group's communal effort and spirit.

- Each set of "Questions for Discussion" includes one that touches on the component of service. This is to keep alive the awareness of the importance of the service aspect, which however is done on the "honor system" (with no one watching over anyone else's shoulder).

Group Etiquette

- Pray for the members of your group be-tween sessions.

- Maintain confidentiality.

- Be a good listener and encourage everyone to contribute to the discussion, without any-one monopolizing. Members that are more talkative should allow everyone a chance to respond before they speak a second time.

- Love your neighbor by speaking charitably and refraining from any kind of gossip.

- Be on time, come prepared, and actively take part in discussion and prayer.

- Take seriously the service component so that you may be a loving (and always hum-ble) witness to the others in your group.

- Be open and expect God's action in your life and prayer—expect to be changed!

Recommended prayer to start each session:

Prayer to the Holy Spirit

Come Holy Spirit,
Fill our hearts with the fire of your love.

Draw us near to Jesus,
so that we may witness to his presence
in every moment of our lives.

Renew us, so that our homes, parishes,
neighborhoods and world
may be transformed into the heavenly
Father's kingdom on earth,
where love and mercy reign.

Amen.

Session 1

Awakening: The Call of Jesus

Jesus in the Scriptures

The Apostle Peter and Awakening / Conversion / Mission

While the people pressed upon [Jesus] to hear the word of God, he was standing by the lake of Gennesaret. And he saw two boats by the lake; but the fishermen had gone out of them and were washing their nets. Getting into one of the boats, which was Simon's, he asked him to put out a little from the land. And he sat down and taught the people from the boat.

And when he had ceased speaking, he said to Simon, "Put out into the deep and let down your nets for a catch." And Simon answered, "Master, we toiled all night and took nothing! But at your word I will let down the nets." And when they had done this, they enclosed a great shoal of fish; and as their nets were breaking, they beckoned to their partners in the other boat to come and help them. And they came and filled both the boats, so that they began to sink.

But when Simon Peter saw it, he fell down at Jesus' knees, saying, "Depart from me, for I am a sinful man, O Lord." For he was astonished, and all that were with him, at the catch of fish which they had taken; and so also were James and John, sons of Zebedee, who were partners with Simon. And Jesus said to Simon, "Do not be afraid; henceforth you will be catching men." And when they had brought their boats to land, they left everything and followed him. **(Luke 5:1-11.)**

Soak in the Word.

Two Minutes of Silence.

Reflect . . .

There are three vital stages of growth that should exist in the life of a committed Christian:

- **Awakening:** Who is Christ and what is my relationship to him?

- **Conversion:** To "convert" comes from Latin and means "to turn." How do I renounce sin and turn radically to Christ, becoming his disciple?

- **Mission:** How can I help bring the love and truth of Christ to others?

It is interesting that in the Bible account of Simon Peter and the great catch of fish, we see evidence of all three of these stages.

Awakening: At the beginning of the account, Simon is washing his nets after a frustrating night of fishing when Jesus asks him to let him teach the crowd from his boat. So Simon puts out from shore and presumably sits next to Jesus while he teaches. What does Jesus teach? The account doesn't tell us, but we know the words of the Son of God penetrate and awaken the hearts of those who are open to the Gospel. Something must be stirring in Peter as he listens to Jesus, because when the miraculous catch of fish occurs, he . . .

Conversion: . . . falls to his knees and says, "Depart from me, Lord, for I am a sinful man." We are so used to reading these words that we may not reflect on the strangeness of the reaction. Why doesn't Peter jump up and down for joy, embrace Jesus, celebrate? Why does his attention suddenly go to his sinfulness? Perhaps because he has been deeply moved by the person of Jesus and his teachings, and senses that he is standing in the presence of extraordinary holiness. Perhaps he feels humbled and even ashamed by contrast, prompting him to want to step away from this radiant light that clashes with the darkness he perceives in his own soul.

Mission: But Jesus tells him not to be afraid, that "from now on you will be catching men." And Peter puts his trust in Jesus, in spite of his own weakness and sinfulness. In fact, the account tells us that he and James and John "left everything and followed him." With the assistance of the Holy Spirit, these men and the other Apostles would become the first evangelizers for Christ.

The Gospels show us that Peter would continue to "awaken," to grow in his awareness and understanding of Jesus.

With his volatile and unreliable nature, he also had much opportunity for continued "conversion," climaxing in his tearful repentance when he denied Christ three times following Jesus' arrest in the Garden of Gethsemane.

Finally, we can all draw encouragement from the fact that this flawed and sinful man ultimately embraced his "mission" as a fervent disciple of Jesus Christ, a powerful evangelizer, the first Pope, and a martyr for the Faith.

Jesus in the Life of His People

Mission Hollywood

Peter, the rough fisherman, was brought to his knees by Jesus' call. He became keenly aware of his sinfulness, his unworthiness, yet Jesus didn't hesitate to call him to a new life and to entrust him with a great mission.

Jesus continues to work in this way. Witness how he touched the life of Eduardo Verástegui, a Mexican pop and television star who made his way to Hollywood in search of money, pleasure and stardom. Stunningly handsome, Eduardo had landed the leading role in *Chasing Papi,* a major motion picture. But he needed to improve his English for the part, so he began working with a tutor.

Eduardo's tutor turned out to be a devout Catholic, and she began to ask him questions like,"Who is God in your life?" "How are you using your talents?" "Do you recognize that your body is a temple of the Holy Spirit?"

When Eduardo told her that he was a Christian and that he loved God, she asked him how this could be, given his self-centered celebrity lifestyle and the kind of acting roles he was taking. Eduardo resisted her loving challenges as long as he could, but one day he found himself alone, thinking about her questions, and suddenly his defenses came crashing down and he realized she was right.

He remembers, "I fell to my knees and started crying like I'd never cried before, and I kept saying, 'Please forgive me.'"

Eduardo made up his mind no longer to accept the kind of Hollywood roles that had typically come his way—roles that stereotyped Latino men as liars, drug dealers or womanizers. "I realized that instead of using my talents to serve and to contribute to a better world, I had been poisoning society by the projects I was involved in." He saw that Hollywood was drawn to the "dark side" of human experience, and instead he "wanted to light a candle" of beauty and hope.

Eduardo credits his conversion to his mother's prayers, recounting that she had said to his father, "Eduardo is lost to us, my words don't touch him anymore. But if my words don't touch him, one day my prayers will." Eduardo believes that is exactly what happened, saying, "Nothing is more powerful than the prayers of a mother."

Soon after this conversion experience, Eduardo

went to a priest, Fr. Juan Rivas, for confession and to seek direction. He began attending daily Mass. He told the priest that he thought he should give up acting and make a mission trip to the jungles of Brazil. The priest told him that Hollywood was a worse "jungle" and needed missionaries even more than Brazil.

But how would he make a living? Where would he find movie roles he could accept?

Eduardo went three years without acting, and it became a struggle just to pay the rent. But Fr. Rivas had told him that God would send like-minded people his way and help him to see the path ahead. Indeed, in 2004 he met two other men, Leo Severino and Alejandro Monteverde, who were in the entertainment business and who, having come back to their own Catholic faith, were eager to do something worthy and beautiful. The "Three Amigos," as they called themselves, worked together with a tiny budget to create the movie *Bella,* a beautiful, life-affirming film that won the 2006 Toronto Film Festival and became a box office success. Even more importantly, a number of women in crisis pregnancies have said that *Bella,* which has a pro-life, pro-adoption theme, moved them to turn away from scheduled abortions and to choose life for their babies.

What was true for St. Peter will no doubt prove true for Eduardo Verástegui—there will be continuing opportunities for awakening, conversion and mission. But already Eduardo evidences a radical commitment to his new life and purpose. As he puts it, "Not only did God forgive me, he made me a new man and he became the center of my life—my Savior, my Creator, my Manager, my Everything."

Catechism of the Catholic Church

1432 - The human heart is heavy and hardened. God must give man a new heart.[1] Conversion is first of all a work of the grace of God who makes our hearts return to him. . . . It is in discovering the greatness of God's love that our heart is shaken by the horror and weight of sin and begins to fear offending God by sin and being separated from him.

[1] Cf. *Ezek* 36:26-27.

Questions for Discussion

1. As Jesus taught from Peter's boat and led him to the great catch of fish, Peter was "awakened" to who Jesus was. When and how are you most aware of the presence of Jesus in your life?

_____

_____

_____

_____

_____

2. Peter was drawn to conversion when Jesus filled his empty net. As you look at your own life, have there been times when frustration or emptiness— or just the realization that earthly things can't fully satisfy you—have prompted you to look more deeply to Christ as the answer? Discuss.

_____

_____

_____

_____

_____

_____

3. Imagine that Jesus appears to you one day, calls you by name and says, "I know you, I know your good qualities, your weaknesses and your sinfulness, and I've got a mission for you. I want you to help me 'catch fish,' catch souls, for the Kingdom of Heaven. You will need to be purified along the way, but trust me and follow me."

- How would you feel? Would you be willing? What would be some of the steps you would want to take to get ready?

- But wait—do you think this personal call from Jesus to you may have already taken place? Think about it and discuss.

_____

_____

_____

_____

_____

_____

_____

4. Peter was a fisherman, with a fisherman's industriousness and determination. Jesus was able to build upon those gifts, making him a "fisher of men." What are some of your gifts and passions that God can use in his service and in the service of your neighbor?

_____

_____

_____

_____

_____

_____

Group Prayers of Intercession

8 to 10 minutes

Closing Prayer

Psalm 139

LORD, you have probed me, you know me:
you know when I sit and stand; you understand my
thoughts from afar.

My travels and my rest you mark; with all my
ways you are familiar.

Even before a word is on my tongue, LORD, you
know it all.

Behind and before you encircle me and rest your
hand upon me.

Such knowledge is beyond me, far too lofty for me
to reach.

Where can I hide from your spirit? From your
presence, where can I flee?

If I ascend to the heavens, you are there; if I lie
down in Sheol, you are there too.

If I fly with the wings of dawn and alight beyond the sea,

Even there your hand will guide me, your right hand hold me fast.

If I say, "Surely darkness shall hide me, and night shall be my light"—

Darkness is not dark for you, and night shines as the day. Darkness and light are but one.

You formed my inmost being; you knit me in my mother's womb. . . .

My very self you knew;. . . .

Probe me, God, know my heart; try me, know my concerns.

See if my way is crooked, then lead me in the ancient paths.

(vv. 1-14, 23-24.)

Session 2

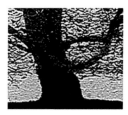

Conversion: Cause for Rejoicing

Jesus in the Scriptures

The Joy of Conversion

[Jesus] entered Jericho and was passing through. And there was a man named Zacchaeus; he was a chief tax collector, and rich. And he sought to see who Jesus was, but could not, on account of the crowd, because he was small of stature. So he ran on ahead and climbed up into a sycamore tree to see him, for he was to pass that way.

And when Jesus came to the place, he looked up and said to him, "Zacchaeus, make haste and come down; for I must stay at your house today." So he made haste and came down, and received him joyfully. And when they saw it they all murmured, "He has gone in to be the guest of a man who is a sinner."

And Zacchaeus stood and said to the Lord, "Behold, Lord, the half of my goods I give to the poor; and if I have defrauded any one of anything, I restore it fourfold."

And Jesus said to him, "Today salvation has come to this house, since he also is a son of Abraham. For the Son of man came to seek and to save the lost."
(Luke 19:1-10.)

Soak in the Word.

Two Minutes of Silence.

Reflect . . .

Many of us may associate conversion first of all with a spirit of repentance, of sorrow for sin. Of course, true conversion cannot take place without repentance and the will to reform, but the story of Zaccheus shows us that what is at the very heart of conversion is first of all something else. For if, as has been noted, to convert means "to turn" away from sin and toward God, it is the turning toward that has primacy. In fact, it's what gives meaning and motivation to turning away from sin in the first place.

How do we see this manifested in the story of Zaccheus? Notice that the first emotion attributed to him when Jesus calls out to him is not pain and sorrow, but joy in having been invited into friendship with Christ. And it is as a consequence of hearing this invitation and turning toward the loving Christ who extends it, that Zaccheus reflects on his own sinfulness and resolves to turn away from it, righting his wrongs through acts of reparation.

It is in beholding and turning toward the glorious light of Jesus Christ, the Son of God, that we become aware of the darkness of sin in our lives and are moved to want to change. If the focus were only on our own sinfulness, we might easily be thrown into depression or even despair. But if we first catch sight of Christ's radiant beauty, if we "taste and see that the Lord is good" *(Psalm 34:8)*, then we can face and repent of our sins with a sense of hope and even joy. Zaccheus, in his joyful and humble encounter with Christ, was far more open to conversion than the grumbling bystanders in their self-righteousness.

Jesus in the Life of His People

The Joyful Breakthrough of Grace

St. Augustine, who lived in the Fourth Century, is regarded as one of the greatest saints in Church history. He is also a "Father" and "Doctor" of the Church because of his profound influence on the articulation of Christian doctrine as it took precise shape in the early centuries.

But Augustine was not always so holy. Indeed, he caused his mother St. Monica quite a lot of worry and tears, and she never stopped praying for him. He had a mistress as a youth and fathered a child by the age of eighteen. He was also proud and ambitious, moving to Milan (the "big city") to make a name for himself as an orator and philosopher. And in this he succeeded.

But despite his celebrity status and much dabbling in the latest philosophical trends, he was left with a feeling of restlessness that nothing seemed able to satisfy.

At last, it seems, the prayers of his mother were answered in the person of St. Ambrose, Bishop of

Milan, who witnessed by word and example to
Christ and the Gospel. After much hesitation and
painful wrestling with the vices he had developed
and found hard to break, Augustine finally opened
himself to true and deep conversion. This conversion
brought him overwhelming joy, which he expressed
in the following poetic passage from his *Confessions:*

> *Late have I loved you, O Beauty ever
> ancient, ever new, late have I loved you! You
> were within me, but I was outside, and it
> was there that I searched for you. . . . Created
> things kept me from you. . . . You called, you
> shouted, and you broke through my deafness.
> You flashed, you shone, and you dispelled my
> blindness. You breathed your fragrance on
> me; I drew in breath and now I pant for you.
> I have tasted you, now I hunger and thirst
> for more. You touched me, and I burned for
> your peace (X, 27, 38).*

Catechism of the Catholic Church

1 - God, infinitely perfect and blessed in himself, in a plan of sheer goodness freely created man to make him share in his own blessed life. For this reason, at every time and in every place, God draws close to man. . . .

142 - . . . "[T]he invisible God, from the fullness of his love, addresses men as his friends, and moves among them, in order to invite and receive them into his own company."[2]

---

[2] *Dei Verbum* 2; cf. *Col* 1:15; *1 Tim* 1:17; *Ex* 33:11; *Jn* 15:14-15; *Bar* 3:38 (Vulg.).

Questions for Discussion

1. Do you think the secular world looks at conversion, and religion in general, as a source of joy? Why or why not?

_____

_____

_____

_____

_____

_____

2. When God approaches us in the midst of our own sinfulness, why should we feel joy and hope? Does this mean that painful feelings like guilt are bad?

_____

_____

_____

_____

_____

_____

3. When you think of conversion, is your first impulse to think more of the turning away from sin, or the turning toward God? Discuss the reasons for your answer.

_____

_____

_____

_____

_____

_____

4. How does serving others bring joy?

_____

_____

_____

_____

_____

_____

5. What does this Bible passage reveal about Jesus,
   about Zaccheus, and about the grumbling bystanders? What lessons can we draw from it?

_____

_____

_____

_____

_____

_____

_____

6. In your spiritual life, your life of faith, can you
   recall some moments of great joy that you might
   share?

_____

_____

_____

_____

_____

7. If Jesus were speaking to you right now, what could he tell you that would give you the greatest possible joy?

_____

_____

_____

_____

_____

_____

Group Prayers of Intercession

8 to 10 minutes

Closing Prayer

Lord God, living and true,
You are love and charity, you are wisdom,

> you are humility, you are patience,
> you are beauty, you are sweetness,
> you are safety, you are rest, you are joy. . .
> you are our life everlasting,
> great and wonderful Lord,
> all powerful God, merciful Savior!
>
> Amen.

(Brief excerpt from a Prayer of Praise of St. Francis of Assisi.)

Session 3

Reconciliation: Repent and Return

Jesus in the Scriptures

The Merciful Father Awaits the Sinner's Return

And [Jesus] said, "There was a man who had two sons; and the younger of them said to his father, 'Father, give me the share of property that falls to me.' And he divided his living between them. Not many days later, the younger son gathered all he had and took his journey into a far country, and there he squandered his property in loose living. And when he had spent everything, a great famine arose in that country, and he began to be in want. So he went and joined himself to one of the citizens of that country, who sent him into his fields to feed swine. And he would gladly have fed on the pods that the swine ate; and no one gave him anything.

But when he came to himself he said, 'How many of my father's hired servants have bread enough and to spare, but I perish here with hunger! I will arise and go to my father, and I will say to him, "Father, I have sinned against heaven and before you; I am no longer worthy to be called your son; treat me as one of your hired servants."' And he arose and came to his father. But while he was yet at a distance, his father saw him and had compassion, and ran and embraced him and kissed him. And the son said to him, 'Father, I have sinned against heaven and before you; I am no longer worthy to be called your son.'

But the father said to his servants, 'Bring quickly the best robe, and put it on him; and put a ring on his hand, and shoes on his feet; and bring the fatted calf and kill it, and let us eat and make merry; for this my son was dead, and is alive again; he was lost, and is found.' **(Luke 15:11-24)**

Soak in the Word.
Two Minutes of Silence.

Reflect . . .

It was a stupid and tragic and sinful thing the prodigal son did. He left the secure, loving environment of his father's house and gave in to a craving for pleasure and the license to do whatever he felt like doing, to "call his own shots." It wasn't until he hit rock bottom, tending pigs (a disgustingly "unclean" animal for the Jews) and wishing he could eat their food, that he came to his senses and regretted deeply the sinful choices he had made. Too late, he thought, to be received back as a son, but maybe his father would take him back as a hired hand. But he had underestimated his father's merciful love and the celebration that would greet his return.

Our story and our fate are not so different. For most of us, our lives in the loving Father's household began with Baptism when we were still newborns. And like the prodigal son, we know what it is to have squandered our inheritance by giving in to our fallen tendencies and making choices that have alienated us from the Father—sinful choices.

Hopefully we have had the grace to do as the prodigal son did in the parable—repent and confess our wrongs, asking for forgiveness. Jesus knew of our need to do this, so when he appeared to the Apostles after his Resurrection, he breathed on them and said, "Receive the Holy Spirit. If you forgive the sins of any, they are forgiven; if you retain the sins of any, they are retained" **(John 20:22-23)**. Thus he instituted the merciful Sacrament of Reconciliation.

Catechism of the Catholic Church

1455 - The confession . . . of sins, even from a simply human point of view, frees us and facilitates our reconciliation with others. Through such an admission man looks squarely at the sins he is guilty of, takes responsibility for them, and thereby opens himself again to God and to the communion of the Church in order to make a new future possible.

1465 - When he celebrates the sacrament of Penance, the priest is fulfilling the ministry of the Good Shepherd who seeks the lost sheep, of the Good Samaritan who binds up wounds, of the Father who awaits the prodigal son and welcomes him on his return, and of the just and impartial judge whose judgment is both just and merciful. . . .

Jesus in the Life of His People

A Modern-Day "Prodigal Daughter"

She has the winning smile and beauty of a super-model. But Leah Darrow calls herself "the poster child for the prodigal daughter."

Born in 1979 on a small farm in Norman, Oklahoma, Leah was the oldest of six children. Her parents were committed Catholics and Leah followed their lead until late high school and college, when "things got fuzzy with my faith."

Speaking at the 2010 Boston Catholic Women's Conference, Leah said of those years, "I did whatever felt good, what was easiest." She bought into the self-centered, worldly culture that surrounded her, and said that during that time "purity, modesty and chastity were things I didn't practice much."

One evening not long after graduating from college, Leah was getting ready to go out with some girlfriends when a TV program caught her eye— "America's Next Top Model." She decided to audition, made it on season three of the show, and got to the final 14 before being eliminated.

Her disappointment just made Leah more determined. She thought to herself, "I'm still going to go after this dream." And so she moved to New York City and little by little found increasing success as a model, to the point where she was making several thousand dollars for an afternoon photo shoot. But she also felt more and more the pull of darkness into which much of the fashion culture leads.

Then came a call from an international glamour magazine. They told Leah they wanted to give her more of a chance to show her sultry, seductive side. She remembers thinking, "You bet!"

So she went to the studio, got her hair and make-up done, and then saw them wheel in a rack of very skimpy outfits. She began to feel embarrassed and afraid, but decided she couldn't show it. She dutifully put on the outfits and the photographer took shot after shot. Thinking back now, she says that a mother looking with her daughter at the photos that ended up in that magazine would say, "See that girl? Don't become like her."

Then, in the middle of the photo shoot, something completely unexpected happened. "Suddenly I saw myself as having died and come to stand before God with my hands extended to him. I was giving him all that he had given me, but my hands were empty because I had wasted all my talents on myself. I had been living the whole past decade for Leah Darrow. He had given me everything for a reason, but it had become wasted talent. I was petrified, ashamed. I knew I couldn't possibly stand there with nothing to offer Christ, when he had given us his whole life."

"You can see in one of the photos from that moment that my skin turned white. The photographer was saying, 'Leah, are you okay?'"

"I just said, 'I can't do this anymore.' I changed back into my clothes and left. I remember walking down the street in New York City just bawling, mascara all down my face, thinking 'what am I doing with my life? I am so unhappy. All the things I wanted I got—my picture in magazines, $16,000 for an afternoon of work—but I'm not happy.'"

Leah went back to her apartment and called her father. She told him, "If you don't come and get me, I'm going to lose my soul."

Her father jumped in the car and drove straight to New York. Leah, depressed at all the ways she had let him down, was afraid to see him, dreading his reaction. But when he finally knocked on the door and she opened it, he looked at her with a big smile and said, "Oh, I am so happy to see you! Let's go to Central Park together! Let's go to the deli! Let's get a hot dog! But first . . . let's get to confession."

And so she did, to a wonderful priest who helped her overcome her initial fears and to unburden herself of "the weight of everything I'd been carrying for years. It's amazing the graces confession gives you."

She would write in her diary, "Satan has had his fun with me for too long. I have been blinded by ignorance and corrupted by vanity and pride. I take back from Satan what is Yours and I give my entire self to You.... Dear Lord, make me new again in You."

Today, Leah works with "Pure Fashion," an international faith-based program that encourages teen girls to live, act, and dress in accordance with their dignity as children of God. She also travels the world bringing hope to others by telling the story of how God changed her life.

In her words, "the best part of my story is not that I was on 'America's Next Top Model,' not that I was a fashion model in New York City. It's that Jesus Christ worked in my life and brought me back from this really bad place and has given me a second chance. That's the best part of my story."

Pope John Paul II

[The] prodigal son is man, every human being: bewitched by the temptation to separate himself from his Father in order to lead his own independent existence; disappointed by the emptiness of the mirage which had fascinated him; alone, dishonored, exploited when he tries to build a world all for himself; sorely tried, even in the depths of his own misery, by the desire to return to communion with his Father. Like the father in the parable, God looks out for the return of his child, embraces him when he arrives and orders the banquet of the new meeting with which the reconciliation is celebrated.

The most striking element of the parable is the father's festive and loving welcome of the returning son: It is a sign of the mercy of God, who is always willing to forgive. Let us say at once: Reconciliation is principally a gift of the heavenly Father.

(Pope John Paul II, *On Reconciliation and Penance, 5.*)

Reflect ...

It took Leah Darrow a long time and a lot of moral mistakes to acknowledge the reality of sin in her life. That is not uncommon in our world today. A certain loss of the sense of sin has led to widespread neglect of the Sacrament of Reconciliation.

Even well-intentioned Catholics who attend Mass faithfully may go to confession only when they are aware of serious sin in their lives, losing sight of the many graces that come from this sacrament even when there are only lighter sins to confess. On October 19, 2005, Pope Benedict XVI spoke to this point in a simple dialogue he had with children making their first Communion. He told them:

> [I]t is very helpful to confess with a certain regularity. It is true: our sins are always the same, but we clean our homes, our rooms, at least once a week, even if the dirt is always the same; in order to live in cleanliness, in order to start again. Otherwise, the dirt might not be seen, but it builds up. Something similar can be said about the soul, for me myself: if I never go to confession, my soul is neglected

and in the end I am always pleased with myself and no longer understand that I must always work hard to improve, that I must make progress. And this cleansing of the soul which Jesus gives us in the Sacrament of Confession helps us to make our consciences more alert, more open, and hence, it also helps us to mature spiritually and as human persons. Therefore, two things: confession is only necessary in the case of a serious sin, but it is very helpful to confess regularly in order to foster the cleanliness and beauty of the soul and to mature day by day in life.

Questions for Discussion

1. Pope John Paul II wrote that the central figure in the parable of the prodigal son is the father, because of the great mercy and forgiveness he shows his repentant son. How aware are you of God's mercy toward you? When are you most aware? Least aware?

_____

_____

_____

_____

_____

_____

2. One could argue that the father in the parable shows the perfect blend of "tough love" and merciful compassion. What is the evidence for each? How does God show us this blend of "tough love" and merciful compassion when we have sinned?

_____

_____

_____

_____

_____

_____

_____

_____

3. When the prodigal son came back repentant from his selfish adventure, his father received him with loving mercy and joy. How might an experience like that increase one's love of neighbor and desire to reach out, to give of oneself?

_____

_____

_____

_____

_____

_____

4. Why do you think people neglect the Sacrament of Reconciliation in our time?

- Do you think you attach sufficient importance to it? If not, perhaps this would be a good time to make some personal resolutions about it.

- What can we do to help reawaken a "healthy" sense of sin?

- Do you think many people understand the simple message quoted above from Pope Benedict XVI's words to the children who had recently made their first Communion?

_____

_____

_____

_____

_____

_____

_____

_____

_____

5. Clearly there are several lessons that can be
drawn from the conversion story of Leah Darrow.
Identify some of them and discuss. Where do you
see her mistakes being repeated in our society, in
ways both large and small (maybe at times even
in yourself)?

_____

_____

_____

_____

_____

_____

_____

_____

_____

_____

_____

_____

Group Prayers of Intercession

8 to 10 minutes

Closing Prayer

Psalm 51

Have mercy on me, O God, according to your stead-
fast love;

according to your abundant mercy blot out my transgressions.

Wash me thoroughly from my iniquity, and cleanse
me from my sin.

For I know my transgressions, and my sin is ever
before me.

Against you, you alone, have I sinned, and done
what is evil in your sight,

so that you are justified in your sentence and blame-
less when you pass judgment. . . .

Purge me with hyssop, and I shall be clean; wash
me, and I shall be whiter than snow.

Let me hear joy and gladness; let the bones that you
have crushed rejoice.

Hide your face from my sins, and blot out all my
iniquities.

Create in me a clean heart, O God, and put a new
and right spirit within me.

(vv. 1-4, 7-10.)

Session 4

The Eucharist: Source of Conversion

Jesus in the Scriptures

Finding Jesus in the Breaking of the Bread

That very day two of them were going to a village named Emmaus, about seven miles from Jerusalem, and talking with each other about all these things that had happened. While they were talking and discussing together, Jesus himself drew near and went with them. But their eyes were kept from recognizing him. And he said to them, "What is this conversation which you are holding with each other as you walk?" And they stood still, looking sad.

Then one of them, named Cleopas, answered him, "Are you the only visitor to Jerusalem who does not know the things that have happened there in these

days?" And he said to them, "What things?" And they said to him, "Concerning Jesus of Nazareth, who was a prophet mighty in deed and word before God and all the people, and how our chief priests and rulers delivered him up to be condemned to death, and crucified him. But we had hoped that he was the one to redeem Israel. Yes, and besides all this, it is now the third day since this happened. Moreover, some women of our company amazed us. They were at the tomb early in the morning and did not find his body; and they came back saying that they had even seen a vision of angels, who said that he was alive. Some of those who were with us went to the tomb, and found it just as the women had said; but him they did not see."

And he said to them, "O foolish men, and slow of heart to believe all that the prophets have spoken! Was it not necessary that the Christ should suffer these things and enter into his glory?" And beginning with Moses and all the prophets, he interpreted to them in all the scriptures the things concerning himself.

So they drew near to the village to which they were going. He appeared to be going further, but they constrained him, saying, "Stay with us, for it is toward evening and the day is now far spent." So he went in to stay with them. When he was at table with them, he took the bread and blessed, and broke it, and gave it to them. And their eyes were opened and they recognized him; and he vanished out of their sight. They said to each other, "Did not our hearts burn within us while he talked to us on the road, while he opened to us the scriptures?" And they rose that same hour and returned to Jerusalem. . . .

(Luke 24:13-33.)

Soak in the Word.

Two Minutes of Silence.

Reflect . . .

Some might say this account, inspiring as it is, is not really about conversion—but look again. The disciples on the road to Emmaus were "packing it in." They were leaving Jerusalem, leaving the holiest city in the world because they had given up. This man Jesus, whom they had hoped would lead Israel back to glory, had died the humiliating death of a criminal, and they had lost all faith in him. They were as empty as Peter's nets before the great catch of fish. They had surrendered to despair.

When were they converted? When did they "turn"? It happened when they recognized Jesus in the breaking of the bread, in the Eucharist. At that moment they turned back to the holy city, back to their brethren, back to faith and hope in Christ.

Pope John Paul II

"Stay with us, Lord, for it is almost evening" **(cf. Lk 24:29)**. This was the insistent invitation that the two disciples journeying to Emmaus on the evening of the day of the resurrection addressed to the Wayfarer who had accompanied them on their journey. Weighed down with sadness, they never imagined that this stranger was none other than their Master, risen from the dead. Yet they felt their hearts burning within them **(cf. v. 32)** as he spoke to them and explained the Scriptures. The light of the Word unlocked the hardness of their hearts and "opened their eyes" **(cf. v. 31)**. Amid the shadows of the passing day and the darkness that clouded their spirit, the Wayfarer brought a ray of light which rekindled their hope and led their hearts to yearn for the fullness of light. "Stay with us," they pleaded. And he agreed. Soon afterwards, Jesus' face would disappear, yet the Master would "stay" with them, hidden in the "breaking of the bread" which had opened their eyes to recognize him.

(Apostolic Letter for the Year of the Eucharist, *Stay With Us, Lord,* 1.)

Jesus in the Life of His People

Lover of the Eucharist, Lover of the Poor

"Stay with us."

These childlike words of the disciples on the road to Emmaus echo in our own hearts, expressing our profound need for Jesus. And the Lord responds, giving himself to us in the wondrous gift of the Eucharist. He also draws near to us through the transparent witness of his saints—holy men and women like St. Martin de Porres.

Martin was born in Lima, Peru in 1579, the illegitimate son of Juan de Porres, a Spanish knight (Spain then controlled most of South America), and Ana Velasquez, a freed African slave. Abandoned at birth by his father—who would later reclaim him at the age of eight—Martin lived in poverty. His mother took in laundry to sustain him and a sister also fathered by Juan.

Martin was kind and compassionate from his earliest years. When his mother sent him with a few coins to buy food at the market in Lima, he would often return late and with the basket empty—having stopped at a church to pray and then given everything away to those who were even more desperately poor. Ana was simultaneously exasperated and impressed by her unusual son.

When his re-emerged father later apprenticed him to the local barber/physician (the two professions overlapped at that time), Martin became quite skilled and a more prosperous future seemed assured. But he had only one desire—to love God perfectly. So at about fifteen years of age he asked the Dominicans of the Monastery of the Holy Rosary to admit him as a lowly servant and member of the Third Order, since people of mixed race were barred from becoming professed members of the community. The Prior of the Monastery already knew Martin's reputation for holiness and accepted him.

Martin rejoiced to embrace the lowliest tasks, sweeping floors and cleaning toilets. That is why pictures and holy cards almost always show him with a broom. But because of his medical skill, he was also put in charge of the infirmary, where he was much beloved. Yet once a priest soured by his ailments began to hurl insults at Martin, saying among other things, "Brother, you shouldn't be in a monastery— you should be in jail!" To the friars who overheard the insults, Martin simply said, "Concerned for my good, this sick priest has set before me my many faults. . . . I agree with his judgment of me."

Martin's spirit of humility and love was fueled by intense devotion to Christ in the Eucharist. When he was not tending the sick, Martin could often be found lost in prayer before the Blessed Sacrament. The friars observed that when he received Holy Communion his face became illuminated "like a burning coal." He also loved to kneel before a large crucifix in one of the common rooms of the monastery where he was frequently seen with his arm outstretched, touching the nailed hand of Christ.

The biographies of St. Martin de Porres recount many astonishing healings and other miracles attributed to him in solemn eyewitness testimony given as early as 1641, only two years after his death.

Let one recurring miracle of charity suffice here. Besides caring for the sick in the monastery, Martin went into the streets to minister to the afflicted and the hungry of Lima. One way he did this was by gathering what food remained after the friars ate dinner and carrying it outside the monastery walls to the waiting throng. He would pray over the food, "May God increase it through his infinite mercy!" His helper, Francis de Santa Fe, testified that at times there was only enough for a few portions, but the kettle was never emptied before everyone had been served.

When Pope John XXIII canonized Martin de
Porres on May 6, 1962, he remarked on his intense
devotion to the Eucharist, his utter humility, and
the name conferred on him by the people of Lima
—"Martin of Charity." He was beloved by people of
every race and status, because he was the loving servant of all. His enduring example and intercession is
one way that Jesus continues even now to "stay with
us," that our hearts may burn with joyful love along
the road of life.

Catechism of the Catholic Church

1394 - As bodily nourishment restores lost
strength, so the Eucharist strengthens our charity,
which tends to be weakened in daily life; and this
living charity wipes away venial sins.[3] By giving
himself to us Christ revives our love and enables us
to break our disordered attachments . . . and root
ourselves in him.

1436 - Daily conversion and penance find their
source and nourishment in the Eucharist, for in it
is made present the sacrifice of Christ which has
reconciled us with God. . . . "It is a remedy to free us
from our daily faults and to preserve us from mortal
sins."[4]

[3] Cf. Council of Trent (1551): DS 1638.
[4] Council of Trent (1551): DS 1638.

Questions for Discussion

1. Read John 6:35-69 (the "Bread of Life" discourse).

- Why did many of Jesus' disciples break away from him after this discourse? Try to put yourself in their shoes as they listened to Jesus.

- What perspective can we bring to Jesus' teaching about eating his body and drinking his blood that they did not have?

_____

_____

_____

_____

_____

_____

_____

_____

_____

2. Probably most Catholics have had moments in which their faith in the great mystery of Jesus' Real Presence in the Eucharist was put to the test. Indeed, when many of his disciples broke away from him after his Bread of Life discourse, Jesus himself put his Apostles to the test, asking them, "Do you also wish to go away? *(John 6:67)*.

- What did Peter say in response?

- What has helped sustain you in your conviction that Jesus is truly present "in the breaking of the bread"?

_____

_____

_____

_____

_____

_____

_____

_____

3. In the Eucharist Jesus gives himself completely to us, and calls us to give of ourselves. One of the anticipated fruits of this faith-sharing experience is service to others. Take some time humbly to share specific ways that members of your group—individually or together—have made an effort to carry this out.

_____

_____

_____

_____

_____

_____

_____

4. More and more parishes today are offering opportunities for Eucharistic adoration. This seems to correspond to an increasing desire for it on the part of many of the faithful.

- Recalling our definition of conversion as turning away from sin and turning toward God, is this hunger for the Eucharist a fruit of conversion or a cause of conversion, or both?

- Besides the mysterious workings of grace, how do you explain this sudden hunger in the midst of our very secular society?

- Have you spent time in prayer before the Blessed Sacrament? If so, what has that meant to you?

_____

_____

_____

_____

_____

_____

_____

_____

_____

_____

_____

_____

_____

_____

Group Prayers of Intercession

8 to 10 minutes

Closing Prayer

Stay with us Lord!

Like the two disciples in the Gospel,
we implore you, Lord Jesus, stay with us!

Divine Wayfarer, expert in our ways
and reader of our hearts, do not leave us
prisoners to the evening shadows.

Sustain us in our weariness, forgive our sins
and direct our steps on the path of goodness. . . .

In the Eucharist, you made yourself the

"medicine of immortality": give us the taste for
a full life that will help us journey on
as trusting and joyful pilgrims on this earth,
our gaze fixed on the goal of life without end.

Stay with us, Lord! Stay with us!

Amen.

**(Pope John Paul II, Opening Mass for the Year of the
Eucharist, October 17, 2004.)**

Session 5

Holiness: Perfection of Charity

Jesus in the Scriptures

The Pathway to Heaven

Seeing the crowds, he went up on the mountain, and when he sat down his disciples came to him. And he opened his mouth and taught them, saying:

"Blessed are the poor in spirit, for theirs is the kingdom of heaven.

"Blessed are those who mourn, for they shall be comforted.

"Blessed are the meek, for they shall inherit the earth.

"Blessed are those who hunger and thirst for righteousness, for they shall be satisfied.

"Blessed are the merciful, for they shall obtain mercy.

"Blessed are the pure in heart, for they shall see God.

80

"Blessed are the peacemakers, for they shall be called sons of God.

"Blessed are those who are persecuted for righteousness' sake, for theirs is the kingdom of heaven.

"Blessed are you when men revile you and persecute you and utter all kinds of evil against you falsely on my account. Rejoice and be glad, for your reward is great in heaven, for so men persecuted the prophets who were before you.

"You are the salt of the earth; but if salt has lost its taste, how shall its saltiness be restored? It is no longer good for anything except to be thrown out and trodden under foot by men.

"You are the light of the world. A city set on a hill cannot be hid. Nor do men light a lamp and put it under a bushel, but on a stand, and it gives light to all in the house. Let your light so shine before men, that they may see your good works and give glory to your Father who is in heaven."

(Matthew 5:1-16.)

Soak in the Word.

Two Minutes of Silence.

Catechism of the Catholic Church

1717 - The Beatitudes depict the countenance of Jesus Christ and portray his charity. They express the vocation of the faithful associated with the glory of his Passion and Resurrection; they shed light on the actions and attitudes characteristic of the Christian life; they are the paradoxical promises that sustain hope in the midst of tribulations. . . .

2013 - "All Christians in any state or walk of life are called to the fullness of Christian life and to the perfection of charity. . . ."[5]

[5] *Lumen Gentium*, 40 § 2.

Pope John Paul II

All the Beatitudes of the Sermon on the Mount indicate the way of conversion and of reform of life *(On the Mercy of God,* 14).
The Beatitudes are not specifically concerned with certain particular rules of behavior. Rather, they speak of basic attitudes and dispositions in life and therefore they do not coincide exactly with the commandments. On the other hand, there is no separation or opposition between the Beatitudes and the commandments: both refer to the good, to eternal life.

(The Splendor of the Truth, 16.)

Reflect . . .

Growth in holiness is a further stage in the process of conversion, of "turning" our lives fully to Christ. Great saints continue in this stage of conversion all their lives, even after the early stages of conversion—turning away from obvious sin—have been pretty well accomplished. Growth in holiness is typically not a matter of performing great acts of heroism, but of accepting the most common of life's daily challenges in the spirit of Christ and the Beatitudes.

Jesus in the Life of His People

St. Thérèse of Lisieux—Daily Trials in Holiness

Perhaps some people think of life in a convent as all peace and roses, but St. Thérèse of Lisieux, the famous "Little Flower," encountered many trials there that challenged her to become even more deeply converted and to grow in holiness. These were the kind of trials that tend to aggravate us all as we live side by side with others in families and communities. What is so extraordinary is the way Thérèse chose to respond when things could have gotten "under her skin." Thankfully she left us her autobiography, *The Story of a Soul,* in which she recounts several of the situations.

One day, Thérèse was laundering handkerchiefs in a wash tub with a group of sisters. One of the sisters splashed the hot, dirty water into her face, over and over again. From childhood Thérèse had struggled with a quick temper, and now it threatened to explode. But with grace and good humor she managed to hold it in check, choosing even "to welcome the shower of dirty water" as a "novel kind of aspersion," and "to come as often as I could to the happy spot where such treasures were freely bestowed." (*The Story of a Soul,* Chapter X.)

Then there was Sister St. Pierre, a crotchety, older nun whose infirmity made it hard for her to keep up with the activities in the monastery. Moved with compassion, Thérèse often took her arm to help her through the hallways. "You are going too fast," the old nun would complain, until Thérèse slowed down. This would prompt a new protest: "Come quicker . . . I cannot feel you . . . you are letting me go!" Then, wrapping up her barrage of complaints, old Sister St. Pierre declared: "I was right when I said you were too young to take care of me" (ibid). No doubt these harsh and ungrateful words stung, but Thérèse managed to hold her tongue and to smile through it all.

Another nun made annoying, clacking noises while the sisters prayed in the chapel. Thérèse does not say what it was, but it is generally assumed that the good sister was fidgeting with her rosary. The repetitive noises threatened to get the best of Thérèse, pounding in her ears. She broke into a sweat trying to shut out the sound, but to no avail. At last, "instead of trying not to hear it, which was impossible, I set myself to listen, as though it had been some delightful music, and my meditation—which was not the 'prayer of quiet'—was passed in offering this music to Our Lord" (ibid).

This is how Thérèse summed up her response to daily trials like these: "Dear Lord, you never tell us to do what is impossible, and yet You can see more clearly than I do how weak and imperfect I am. If, then, You tell me to love my sisters as You love them, that must mean that You Yourself must go on loving them in and through me. You know it wouldn't be possible any other way. . . ." (*The Story of a Soul*, Chapter IX.)

St. Francis of Assisi—Heroic Sanctity

In their ordinariness and simplicity, the anecdotes about St. Thérèse are encouraging, in that they remind us that holiness is found mostly in meeting day-to-day events with the love of Christ in our hearts. But occasionally we may face circumstances in which holiness calls for a higher degree of heroism. The following excerpt from a biography of St. Francis of Assisi illustrates the point:

> As with all other cities, there was also in the vicinity of Assisi a lepers' hospital. . . . On his walks in this place, Francis now and then passed by the hospital, but the mere sight of it had filled him with horror. He would not even give an alms to a leper unless someone else would take it for him. Especially when the wind blew from the hospital, and the weak, nauseating odor, peculiar to the leper, came across the road, he would hurry past with averted face and fingers in his nostrils.
> (Jorgensen, Johannes, *St. Francis of Assisi*, Doubleday Image, 1939, p. 38.)

Then, one day, Francis was out riding horseback, when he saw a leper ahead of him on the road.

Francis started, and even his horse shared in the movement, and his first impulse was to turn and flee as fast as he could. . . .

. . . [W]ith a mighty victory over himself, Francis sprang from his horse, approached the leper, from whose deformed countenance the awful odor of corruption issued forth, placed his alms in the outstretched wasted hand—bent down quickly and kissed the fingers of the sick man, covered with the awful disease, whilst his system was nauseated with the action. . . . When he again sat upon his horse, he hardly knew how he had got there. He was overcome by excitement. . . . Sweetness, happiness, and joy streamed into his soul. . . . **(Jorgenson, p. 39.)**

Questions for Discussion

1. In his letter *At the Beginning of the New Millennium,* Pope John Paul II called on the faithful to "contemplate the face of Christ." He said that an intense focus on religious programs and activities would be fruitless if we did not first give priority to such contemplation. Does this message "resonate" with you? How would you explain it to someone who asked you to help them understand?

_____

_____

_____

_____

_____

_____

2. In his first encyclical, *Deus Caritas Est* (God is Love), Pope Benedict XVI wrote, "Love of God and love of neighbor have become one: in the least of the brethren we find Jesus himself, and in Jesus we find God" **(n. 15)**. Yet, in the anecdote about St. Francis we saw how difficult it was for this good and holy man to embrace Christ in the leper.

- What makes it so difficult to recognize and embrace Christ in others?

- What do we need to overcome that difficulty?

_____

_____

_____

_____

_____

_____

_____

_____

_____

3. Read the Ten Commandments **(Exodus 20:1-17).**
   Then read the Beatitudes that begin this session
   (Matthew 5:1-16). Both have to do with conversion,
   with turning away from sin and toward God. How
   are they distinct from each other, starting with
   the difference in the way they are stated?

   _____

   _____

   _____

   _____

   _____

   _____

4. "Holiness" is a word that actually rubs many people the wrong way. It can strike them as boring and disconnected from "real life" (all harps and clouds and hymns and angel wings).

- Why do you suppose that is?

- What would you say is the correct, attractive understanding of holiness?

- Who are some people who have been appealing examples of that?

_____

_____

_____

_____

_____

_____

_____

_____

_____

5. Jesus tells us we are "the salt of the earth" and "the light of the world." What are the purposes of salt and light, and what does that tell us about our mission?

_____

_____

_____

_____

_____

_____

_____

_____

Group Prayers of Intercession

8 to 10 minutes

Closing Prayer

Radiating Christ

Dear Jesus, help me to spread your fragrance everywhere I go.

Flood my soul with your spirit and life.

Penetrate and possess my whole being so utterly that my life may only be a radiance of yours.

Shine through me and be so in me that every soul I come in contact with may feel your presence in my soul.

Let them look up and see no longer me, but only Jesus.

Stay with me and then I shall begin to shine as you shine, so to shine as to be a light to others.

The light, O Jesus, will be all from you.

None of it will be mine.

It will be you shining on others through me.

Let me thus praise you in the way you love best by
   shining on those around me.

Let me preach you without preaching,

   not by words, but by my example;
   by the catching force,
   the sympathetic influence,
   of what I do,
   the evident fullness of the love
   my heart bears to you.

Amen.

**(Adapted prayer of Cardinal John Henry Newman.
Prayed daily by Blessed Mother Teresa's Missionaries of
Charity.)**

Session 6

Redemption: By His Stripes We Are Healed

Jesus in the Scriptures

The Prophet Isaiah and our Salvation Foretold

Who has believed what we have heard? And to whom has the arm of the LORD been revealed? For he grew up before him like a young plant, and like a root out of dry ground; he had no form or comeliness that we should look at him, and no beauty that we should desire him. He was despised and rejected by men; a man of sorrows, and acquainted with grief; and as one from whom men hide their faces he was despised, and we esteemed him not.

Surely he has borne our griefs and carried our sorrows; yet we esteemed him stricken, smitten by God, and afflicted. But he was wounded for our transgressions, he was bruised for our iniquities; upon him was the chastisement that made us whole,   and with his stripes we are healed. All we like sheep have gone astray; we have turned every one to his own way; and the LORD has laid on him the iniquity of us all.

He was oppressed, and he was afflicted, yet he opened not his mouth; like a lamb that is led to the slaughter, and like a sheep that before its shearers is dumb, so he opened not his mouth. By oppression and judgment he was taken away; and as for his generation, who considered that he was cut off out of the land of the living, stricken for the transgression of my people? And they made his grave with the wicked and with a rich man in his death, although he had done no violence, and there was no deceit in his mouth.

Yet it was the will of the LORD to bruise him; he has put him to grief; an offering for sin, he shall see his offspring, he shall prolong his days; the will of the LORD shall prosper in his hand; he shall see the fruit of the travail of his soul and be satisfied; by his knowledge shall the righteous one, my servant, make many to be accounted righteous; and he shall bear their iniquities. Therefore I will divide him a portion with the great, and he shall divide the spoil with the strong; because he poured out his soul to death, and was numbered with the transgressors; yet he bore the sin of many, and made intercession for the transgressors. *(Isaiah 53:1-12)*

The Arrival of the Lamb

The next day [John the Baptist] saw Jesus coming toward him, and said, "Behold, the Lamb of God, who takes away the sin of the world!"
(John 1:29)

Adam's Curse Reversed

. . . [D]eath reigned from Adam to Moses, even over those whose sins were not like the transgression of Adam. . . . But the free gift is not like the trespass. For if many died through one man's trespass, much more have the grace of God and the free gift in the grace of that one man Jesus Christ abounded for many. . . . For as by one man's disobedience many were made sinners, so by one man's obedience many will be made righteous. *(Rom 5:14-15,19)*

Redemption Proclaimed

"Let all the house of Israel therefore know assuredly that God has made him both Lord and Christ, this Jesus whom you crucified." Now when they heard this they were cut to the heart, and said to Peter and the rest of the apostles, "Brethren, what shall we do?" And Peter said to them, "Repent, and be baptized every one of you in the name of Jesus Christ for the forgiveness of your sins; and you shall receive the gift of the Holy Spirit. *(Acts 2:36-38)*

Soak in the Word.

Two Minutes of Silence.

Reflect . . .

To redeem means to "buy back." Jesus purchased us back from slavery to sin, a slavery into which the human race had fallen thanks to the original sin of our first parents. He paid our debt of sin at great cost to himself, by his loving sacrifice on the Cross. He bought us with the currency of love—"Greater love has no man than this, that a man lay down his life for his friends" *(John 15:13).*

That love, that currency, has been deposited for each of us, and it is Baptism that draws on the account, draws on the Redemption won by Christ. It is through our Baptism that we are personally purchased by the grace and love of Christ and invited to live in that love.

The redeeming power of sacrificial love is seen first of all in Christ, but then also in those who join their loving sacrifice to his, as we shall see in the following illustration. . . .

Jesus in the Life of His People

The Mystery of Redemptive Love in Suffering

In his book *A Severe Mercy,* author Sheldon Vana-uken tells a story of love and conversion. He and his beloved wife Davy, a bright, adventurous and unbelieving couple, meet the Christian writer C.S. Lewis and eventually convert to Christianity. But Davy's conversion runs deeper than Sheldon's, who wistfully dreams of sailing the open seas with Davy as they had done before knowing Christ. He writes:

> But, though I wouldn't have admitted it, even to myself, I didn't want God aboard. He was too heavy. I wanted Him approving from a considerable distance. I didn't want to be thinking of Him. I wanted to be free. . . . I wanted life itself, the colour and fire and loveliness of life. And Christ now and then, like a loved poem I could read when I wanted to. I didn't want to be swallowed up in God. I wanted holidays from the school of Christ. . . . But for Davy, to live was Christ. . . .

> And Davy one night, having contemplated holiness, said she was restless and would

sleep in the guestroom. But she did not sleep: she prayed. All night, like the saints, she wrestled in prayer. Some say that prayer, even prayer for what God desires, releases power by the operation of a deep spiritual law; and to offer up what one loves may release still more. However that may be, Davy that night offered up her life. For me—that my soul might be fulfilled. . . ."
(Vanauken, Sheldon, *A Severe Mercy,* Harper & Row, 1977, pp.134-135, 145.)

And so it happens that Davy contracts a terminal illness and eventually dies, and Sheldon is drawn closer to Christ (later he would enter the Catholic Church). Did God join Davy's sacrifice to that of his only-begotten Son for the deeper conversion of Sheldon? Perhaps, for consider what St. Paul wrote in his first letter to the Colossians: "Now I rejoice in my sufferings for your sake, and in my flesh I complete what is lacking in Christ's afflictions for the sake of his body, that is, the church" **(1:24).**

Pope John Paul II commented on this mysterious passage in his letter *On the Christian Meaning of Human Suffering*. There he explained that this doesn't literally mean that Christ's sufferings for our redemption were inadequate. No, but Christ has nonetheless chosen—freely and without necessity—to let us participate in his redeeming sacrifice by joining our sufferings to his, across all time and space. This doesn't mean we should go looking for suffering (Davy's self-offering for Sheldon was exceptional, not the norm), but when it comes our way we can consciously ask Christ to let us join it to his sacrifice for our own good and the good of others. What a powerful source of hope and meaning this can be, especially when disease or advanced age or some other debilitating condition makes people feel useless or burdensome.

Our Need for Continued Conversion

Unfortunately, even after Christ's redeeming grace has entered us in Baptism, the world of sin tries to seduce us back into slavery. Like Sheldon Vanauken, we are familiar with that backward pull, that tug. Because, even though Baptism cleanses us of sin, the effects of original sin remain in our fallen nature: weakness in our mind and will, along with disordered desires. These are not themselves sinful, but they incline us to sin. And so we experience tendencies toward selfishness, pride, jealousy, lust, revenge, etc. This struggle is captured by St. Paul in his Letter to the Romans:

> For I do not do the good I want, but the evil I do not want is what I do. . . . So I find it to be a law that when I want to do right, evil lies close at hand. For I delight in the law of God, in my inmost self, but I see in my members another law at war with the law of my mind and making me captive to the law of sin which dwells in my members. Wretched man that I am! Who will deliver me from this body of death? Thanks be to God through Jesus Christ our Lord! *(Rom 7:19, 21-25.)*

Catechism of the Catholic Church

1426 - Conversion to Christ, the new birth of Baptism, the gift of the Holy Spirit and the Body and Blood of Christ received as food have made us "holy and without blemish. . . ."[6] Nevertheless the new life received in Christian initiation has not abolished the frailty and weakness of human nature . . . which remains in the baptized such that with the help of the grace of Christ they may prove themselves in the struggle of Christian life.[7]

[6] *Eph* 1:4; 5:27.
[7] Cf. Council of Trent (1546): DS 1515.

Questions for Discussion

1. Probably most of us can relate to the way Sheldon Vanauken felt about Christ—wanting Him "now and then, like a loved poem" he could read when he wished to, wanting "holidays from the school of Christ."

   - Why are we like that? Why are we resistant to being "swallowed up in God"?

   - What is the antidote to that kind of thinking?

   _____

   _____

   _____

   _____

   _____

   _____

   _____

   _____

2. Sheldon Vanauken became acutely aware that his wife Davy had literally offered her life for him. How aware are you that Jesus offered his life for you personally (not just for "mankind" in some generic way)?

_____

_____

_____

_____

3. There is an acceptable theological opinion that says Jesus could have redeemed us through the shedding of even one drop of his precious blood (or some other act of loving sacrifice), but that he embraced the extreme of a humiliating and agonizing death for us. If this view is true, what might have been the purpose of choosing such an excruciating path?

_____

_____

_____

_____

_____

4. Discuss both the joys and the challenges of the service aspect of this faith-sharing experience. How has this way of living the faith impacted your life?

_____

_____

_____

_____

_____

_____

_____

_____

5. When the pagans witnessed the example of the early Christians, they were moved to say, "See how they love one another." After this experience of shared faith and prayer leading to service, can you envision small groups like yours helping to bring about significant renewal in parishes and even dioceses as a whole? Discuss.

_____

_____

_____

_____

_____

_____

Group Prayers of Intercession

8 to 10 minutes

Closing Prayer

Lord Jesus Christ, eternal king,

God and man, crucified for mankind,

look upon me with mercy and hear my prayer,

for I trust in you.

Have mercy on me, full of sorrow and sin,

for the depth of your compassion never ends.

Praise to you, saving sacrifice,

offered on the wood of the cross for me

and for all mankind.

Praise to the noble and precious blood,

flowing from the wounds of my crucified Lord Jesus
Christ
and washing away the sins of the whole world.

Remember, Lord, your creature,
whom you have redeemed with your blood.
Amen.

(From a Fourth Century prayer of St. Ambrose for Preparation before Mass.)

Appendix

Suggestions for Service

As stated in the Introduction, we are not truly disciples of Christ until we take seriously his words: "Truly, I say to you, as you did it to one of the least of these my brethren, you did it to me" **(Matthew 25:40).**

With a smile and an open heart, we are called to be the hands and feet of Christ in the world, especially to those in need. But sometimes we need a little help getting started. Here are a few suggestions:

Ask your pastor about needs in the parish community

"Charity begins at home," and in the life of the Church that's your parish. Your pastor can help you learn who are the lonely, the elderly, the sick or homebound in your community. He can tell you who needs Holy Communion, the human kindness of a visit, and who has material needs. You might also ask if there are parishioners who need a ride to Mass because of age, health, or special needs.

Contact Catholic Charities

Consider offering some volunteer time

to Catholic Charities, which has agencies throughout the country. To find one near you, visit **www.catholiccharitiesusa. org,** click on "Who We Are" and then "Local Agency Directory."

Check your Yellow Pages listings under "Social Service Organizations" or "Volunteer Services"

You may be surprised to learn how many opportunities for service exist in your community: Meals on Wheels, Habitat for Humanity, Birthright or other crisis pregnancy centers, food pantries, homeless shelters, Catholic Worker houses, and more.

Pay attention to what is "right under your nose"

Sometimes we can get tied up in a knot trying to decide where to go and what to do, when there's an elderly neighbor next door or a nursing home a few blocks away. No doubt, there are people close by that are lonely and would love a visit.

May the ancient witness be renewed:

"See how they love one another!"

The Discipleship Series

Novo Millennio Press